Contents

Preface

In June of 2007, I deployed to Naval Station Guantanamo Bay, Cuba. There I served in the Office for the Administrative Review of the Detention of Enemy Combatants (OARDEC). This organization is responsible for conducting Combatant Status Review Tribunals (CSRTs) and Administrative Review Boards (ARBs) on those individuals detained during the Global War on Terrorism. I served as a member of a three person ARB. Our duty was to conduct an annual review of the status of each enemy combatant. Specifically, we analyzed the threat and intelligence value of the detainees and made recommendations to the Deputy Secretary of Defense on their continued detention.

While serving in this position, I often thought about the controversy that surrounded Guantanamo Bay and wondered what the United States would do if it did not have Guantanamo Bay as an option for a detention location. When I learned that both candidates for the 2008 Presidential Election favored closing Guantanamo Bay's detention facility, I wanted to look further to determine if this was a good or bad idea. More importantly, I wanted to find out what the options are for the remaining detainees. During the course of my research, President Barack Obama quickly ordered the closure of Guantanamo Bay. Once I learned the fate of Guantanamo Bay, I was eager to find out what the U.S. must do to make it happen.

Abstract

After September 11, 2001, the United States began a global campaign to eliminate terrorists and their support networks. During the Global War on Terror, President George Bush established the detention facility at Guantanamo Bay, Cuba to hold individuals captured during military operations in Afghanistan and Iraq. From the very beginning, Guantanamo Bay has faced criticism throughout the world. The Bush administration was ill prepared to begin and sustain detainee operations and failed to properly classify detainees under the Geneva Conventions. Subsequently, the Administration developed questionable legal processes for the detainees by capitalizing on the "legal-free" environment offered at Guantanamo Bay, which led many to call for the closure of the detention facility. After only two days in office, President Barack Obama ordered the closure of Guantanamo Bay and a review of all detainees to ensure proper classification, prosecution, and need for continued detention. Is the closure of Guantanamo Bay necessary or is the problem the policy and procedures regarding the detainees and the conditions of their detention? This paper presents the history of the classification and legal processes that faced the detainees since the first days of Guantanamo Bay. It then analyzes the arguments for keeping it open and closing it down and it examines the future steps required to close Guantanamo Bay in accordance with President Obama's executive order. Finally, it offers recommendations on how the U.S. can properly handle the disposition of detainees, to include legal due process in the U.S. criminal justice system, while still utilizing the detention center at Guantanamo Bay. Closing Guantanamo Bay is the wrong answer. The U.S. must revamp the its methods for dealing with detainees during the GWOT and for any future military campaigns.

Section I

Introduction

In September of 2001, the United States endured one of the most catastrophic events in the nation's history. These terrorist attacks sent a shockwave throughout the entire world. The United States found itself facing a challenging type of enemy: terrorists. Once combat operations began in Afghanistan and Iraq, the U.S. detained many individuals for interrogation and held them indefinitely if they continued to pose a risk to the United States or the rest of the world. The fundamental reason for detaining these individuals was to keep them from rejoining the fight. As such, the U.S. chose to create a detention facility at the Naval Station in Guantanamo Bay, Cuba. By June of 2002, the U.S. had transferred over 500 Taliban and al Qaida fighters to Guantanamo Bay.[1] As of December of 2008, that number had decreased to approximately 250 detainees to include 15 "high-value" detainees.[2]

Throughout the last six years of operation, Guantanamo Bay has faced endless criticism from the international community and from home. Most criticized is the legal "black hole" that exists at Guantanamo Bay and concern over interrogation techniques and torture. In the latter years of his presidency, George W. Bush stated his desire to eventually close the detention facility. In addition, both presidential candidates John McCain and Barack Obama pledged to close the facility if elected. After winning the election, President Barack Obama stated that closing Guantanamo Bay was a top priority for his administration.[3] Obviously, this initiative will please many and upset others. However, should the U.S. close Guantanamo Bay? If so, what will the U.S. do with the remaining detainees? What are the alternatives to detention at Guantanamo Bay? These critical questions require a thorough analysis.

It is easy to claim that Guantanamo Bay should close its cells forever. After all, it created endless controversy and continues damaging the reputation of the United States throughout the international community. Does the facility create this unfavorable stigma? Alternatively, is the underlying problem the way in which the United States handled these detainees from the start? Perhaps the process needs attention and not the fact that the detainees are isolated on a Caribbean island. The primary concern of Guantanamo Bay is the legal vacuum that exists. The process by which the U.S. determined the detention status of detainees and the policy and procedures used to continue their detention is the culprit. President Obama must quickly address this problem and revamp these processes to ensure the United States can create a new honorable and moral standard for the remainder of the Global War on Terrorism.

Detainee operations at Guantanamo Bay continue to cast a dark cloud over the United States and its pursuit in the Global War on Terrorism. Using the problem/solution method of research, this paper will discuss the argument surrounding the detention facility at Guantanamo Bay. It will first consider the background on Guantanamo Bay by discussing the history of the classification of detainees, the reason for choosing Guantanamo Bay, and the current legal process used for the detainees. Next, it will examine the arguments for both closing Guantanamo Bay down and keeping it open. It will then evaluate some alternatives to Guantanamo Bay. Finally, it will conclude with recommendations for solving these issues at Guantanamo Bay.

President Obama should not close the detention facility at Guantanamo Bay. The problem is not the location of the detention facility. Given the amount of resources expended to develop this facility, it would not be to simply shut it down and walk away. The problem began with the Bush administration's failure to prepare for the detainment of those individuals capture during military operations in Afghanistan and Iraq. This lack of preparation combined with the adhoc nature in which the administration created policy and procedures for detainees is the true source of the last six years of controversy. To make detainee operations at Guantanamo Bay fair, legal and morally adequate, the Obama administration must revise the current policy and procedures. Only then can Guantanamo Bay continue to operate in a manner acceptable to the U.S. and the international community.

Section II

Why Guantanamo Bay?

Why Guantanamo Bay Was Chosen

Situated in the Caribbean in the southeastern tip of Cuba is Guantanamo Bay Naval Base. The United States began leasing this area back in 1903 making it the oldest overseas U.S. Navy base.[4] In the early 1990s, Haitian and Cuban migrants overran the base. During this period, the base constructed the now infamous Camp X-Ray as a temporary holding facility for these migrants. By the end of the decade, the base released the migrants and only held Chinese migrants intercepted while trying to sneak into the U.S.[5] In January of 2002, United States Southern Command received orders to take custody of detainees picked up during military operations in Central Command and hold them at Guantanamo Bay for detention and further disposition.[6] Guantanamo Bay allowed the U.S. an area to establish a detention facility in a secure and isolated location eliminating any chance the detainees would rejoin the fight. In addition, Guantanamo Bay allowed the U.S. to avoid bringing those individuals suspected of terrorism from entering domestic soil. Camp X-Ray was the only remaining facility from the 1990s migrations and used as a temporary holding facility for detainees brought to Guantanamo Bay. Thus, began the history of detainee operations at Guantanamo Bay. Immediately there was concern over the conditions at Camp X-Ray. In January of 2004, the Red Cross visited Camp X-Ray to evaluate the conditions at the facility.[7] It was determined that the detainees were well fed, provided correct dietary meals, and given access to shower and toilet facilities.[8] However, concerns came flooding in once pictures surfaced illustrating the mistreatment and abuse of some detainees at Camp X-Ray by military guards. This resulted in an international outcry to examine and address the conditions of detention at Guantanamo Bay. It is here that the world began discovering the reasons behind why the U.S. chose Guantanamo Bay.

The United States never formally declared war after the attacks of September 11, 2001. How could it have declared war? When the Bush administration began military operations following 9/11, it named terrorism as the enemy. As such, the Global War on Terror (GWOT) began. Throughout history, the U.S. has fought against a specified enemy. Whether it was the German armies or the Vietcong, the U.S. knew precisely who its enemy was. Today, we fight against a tactic, not an identifiable enemy. Webster's online dictionary defines terrorism as "the systematic use of violence as a means to intimidate or coerce societies or governments".[9] It becomes immediately obvious that classifying individuals suspected of terrorism is a difficult challenge at best. Therefore, the President, using his constitutional authority, issued a military order to authorize detention, treatment, and trial of non-citizens during the GWOT campaign.[10] A leaked classified report, prepared by the Department of Defense, offers insight as to why Guantanamo Bay became the choice for detainee operations. The report claimed that Guantanamo Bay offered the Bush administration certain legal "advantages" because its location fell outside of U.S. court jurisdiction.[11] This offered the U.S. the ability to detain individuals and conduct interrogations with minimal influence of U.S. legal policy and procedures. However, this murky situation created dissent among many across the international community as the legal black hole at Guantanamo Bay took hold. Understanding this controversy requires a discussion

of the background and evolution of the classification of the detainees.

History of the Classification, Policy, and Procedures for Detainees

One of the most significant factors contributing to the legal vacuum at Guantanamo Bay

is the classification of the detainees. This had been a constant source of controversy and

confusion on behalf of the Bush administration. Originally, Secretary of Defense Donald

Rumsfeld identified the detainees as "unlawful combatants" with no rights under the Geneva

Conventions.[12] However, Rumsfeld indicated that the U.S. would treat detainees consistent with

the Geneva Conventions. By taking this approach, the Bush administration claimed that these

individuals are unlawful combatants and not military soldiers. This distinction is important

because it allowed the U.S. to hold detainees for the duration of hostilities during the GWOT

while also denying them prisoner of war status since that is only offered to lawful combatants.[13]

Finally, this allowed the U.S. to prosecute the detainees for not only war crimes, but also for

ordinary military action since they are not given combatants privilege.[14] This position coupled

with images of the detainees shackled and wearing blacked-out goggles instigated an outcry from

human rights organizations across the globe. A unilateral decision that the Geneva Conventions

did not protect these individuals led many to fear that the U.S. could face greater criticism from

across the globe, not to mention the increased risk that U.S. troops might face while fighting in

Afghanistan. In response, Bush adjusted his position stating that Taliban fighters were now

protected under the Geneva Conventions, but still not considered prisoners of war since they

failed to meet the requirements as lawful combatants under international standards.[15] Bush also

stated that al Qaida fighters were still outside of the protections of the Geneva Conventions since it is not a state or a party to the treaty.[16] However, the U.S. Supreme Court ruled in *Hamdan v Rumsfeld* that the military commissions were in violation of the Geneva conventions.[17] In addition, al Qaida fighters received rights in accordance with the Geneva Conventions.[18]

It is important to stop here and recognize that the Bush administration's failure to properly plan for the detention of enemy fighters during combat operations began the legal controversy surrounding Guantanamo Bay. Had the administration properly applied the Geneva Conventions prior to military operations in Afghanistan, it could have addressed the proper classification of detainees apprehended on the battlefield. Many argued, to include the Bush administration, that the U.S. was not fighting traditional military soldiers and therefore the Geneva Conventions were not applicable. This is simply not true. Article 4 of the Third Convention provides quite clear guidance:

> Prisoners of war, in the sense of the present Convention, are persons belonging to one of the following categories, who have fallen into the power of the enemy: (1) Members of the armed forces of a Party to the conflict, as well as members of militias or volunteer corps forming part of such armed forces. (2) Members of other militias and members of other volunteer corps, including those of organized resistance movements, belonging to a Party to the conflict and operating in or outside their own territory, even if this territory is occupied, provided that such militias or volunteer corps, including such organized resistance movements, fulfill the following conditions: (a) that of being commanded by a person responsible for his subordinates; (b) that of having a fixed distinctive sign recognizable at a distance; (c) that of carrying arms openly; (d) that of conducting their operations in accordance with the laws and customs of war. (3) Members of regular armed forces who profess allegiance to a government or an authority not recognized by the Detaining Power.[19]

This guidance is appropriate for the Taliban, but al Qaida fighters are more difficult to consider.

Fortunately, Article 5 of the Third Convention resolves this potential issue:

> The present Convention shall apply to the persons referred to in Article 4 from the time they fall into the power of the enemy and until their final release and repatriation.

Should any doubt arise as to whether persons, having committed a belligerent act and having fallen into the hands of the enemy, belong to any of the categories enumerated in Article 4, such persons shall enjoy the protection of the present Convention until such time as their status has been determined by a competent tribunal.

Clearly, the Bush administration could and should have granted POW status per the Geneva Conventions to detainees until further classified. Failing to use this guidance allowed the legal black hole at Guantanamo Bay to persist until the U.S. Supreme Court made some significant rulings over the course of the last four years.

The first significant case is *Rasul v. Bush* in which the Supreme Court ruled that Guantanamo Bay is, for all intents and purposes, a U.S. territory and therefore the detainees there have habeas corpus rights allowing them to challenge their detention in court.[20] Until this point, detainees sat in a vacuum without the ability to contest the reasons for their detention. In response, the Bush administration stood up the Office for the Administration of the Detention of Enemy Combatants (OARDEC) and developed the Combatant Status Review Tribunals (CSRT) and Administrative Review Boards (ARB). The three-person CSRT panel would listen to evidence on each detainee and determine whether the detainee meets the criteria of an enemy combatant.[21] OARDEC conducted CSRTs on all detainees with the exception of the fourteen "high-value detainees." Thirty-eight detainees failed to meet the criteria for enemy combatants and 23 of them were transferred back to their home states.[22] In 2007, the fourteen "high-value detainees" went through the CSRT process and deemed enemy combatants and of those individuals, only one went through the military commissions process.[23] Once designated as an enemy combatant, the detainee then faced an annual ARB to review the evidence against him. Specifically, the ARB reviews the evidence to determine if the detainee still poses a threat to the U.S. or its friends and allies. In addition, the ARB determines whether the detainee is of continued intelligence value. The first round of ARBs resulted in the release of 14 detainees, transfer of 120 detainees, and continued detention for 329 detainees.[24]

Also from *Rasul v. Bush*, the administration developed the Detainee Treatment Act of 2005 and the Military Commissions Act of 2006. The Detainee Treatment Act prohibited mistreatment and abuse of detainees and implemented a uniform standard operating procedure for the conduct of interrogations. It also removed federal court jurisdiction over challenges from detainees regarding the conditions of their internment.[25] By sneaking this last item of legislation, the Bush administration was able to sidestep the mechanism for detainee due process.

The next significant Supreme Court ruling came out of *Hamdan v. Rumsfeld*, in which the court ruled the proposed military commissions for Guantanamo detainees were illegal in accordance with domestic and international law. Not to be outdone, the administration once again proposed new legislation to address this court ruling through the Military Commissions Act of 2006. This bill gave Bush the ability to set up military commissions to try detainees. In addition, it reiterated the inability for detainees to challenge their detention and blocked any attempt by the detainee to prevent hearsay evidence against them.[26] Finally, this bill created the definition of an unlawful enemy combatant: "a person who has engaged in hostilities or has purposefully and materially supported hostilities against the U.S. or is co-belligerents who is not a lawful enemy combatant (including a person who is part of the Taliban, al Qaida, or associated forces); or a person who has been determined to be an unlawful enemy combatant by a CSRT or another competent tribunal established under the authority of the President or the Secretary of Defense".[27] Once again, the Guantanamo black hole resurfaces and holds steady until another Supreme Court ruling.

In the case of *Boumediene v. Bush*, the Supreme Court struck down the Military Commissions Act provision that had again stripped detainees of their habeas corpus rights calling it unconstitutional.[28] It is important to understand that this ruling does not eliminate the military commissions. What is does is allow detainees to challenge whether or not they should have been classified as an enemy combatant in the first place. In a case consolidated with *Boumediene v. Bush*, the case of *Al Odah v. United States*, CSRT panel member Lieutenant Colonel Stephen Abraham, an Air Force intelligence officer, provided an alarming testimony concerning detainee operations at Guantanamo Bay. Lt Col Abraham testified that the CSRTs were nothing more than a dog and pony show that relied upon generic evidence allowing the panels to quickly rubber stamp detainees as enemy combatants.[29] This no doubt struck a chord with the Supreme Court and proved compelling enough to assist the Court in overturning its decision thus agreeing to hear cases. Since then, the CSRT and Administrative Review Board (ARB) processes continue to draw criticism for their lack of credible legal sufficiency and due process. There have been no further Supreme Court decisions, thus the current process remains unaltered as of January 2009.

Today, there is a new idea for dealing with the Guantanamo Bay detainees. If the U.S. is not going to try the detainee for war crimes and has chosen not to release him, he should be held under the title of "preventive detention." Under this philosophy, the detainees are held, possibly indefinitely, not because of what they did, but because of what the U.S. suspects they may attempt if released.[30] If implemented, this approach would simply illustrate another government attempt at misdirection concerning the necessity for holding detainees during throughout the GWOT. This will remain an issue for President Obama to consider since he inherited the

Guantanamo Bay problem. Although Bush often stated that he wanted to close Guantanamo Bay, he knew that doing so would be an incredibly difficult and time-consuming challenge.

Based on the Bush administration's rationale for choosing Guantanamo Bay for detainee operations and the subsequent Supreme Court rulings to legitimize the process, it becomes clear this concept of operations was fundamentally flawed from the onset of the Global War on Terrorism. The Bush administration failed to plan appropriately to handle the disposition of detainees captured on the battlefield. There is no doubt these detainees had the potential to cause great harm to the U.S. and its friends and required removal from the fight. As such, the Bush administration needed to give POW treatment to Taliban and al Qaida fighters until properly classified under the Geneva Conventions. Unilaterally determining that all detainees were enemy combatants was a mistake. The plethora of legal battles and Supreme Court rulings over the past four years provides proof of this invalid determination under domestic and international law. Unfortunately, the Bush administration believed its handling of Guantanamo Bay detainees was the right approach all along even in the face of all the adversity and legal battles.[31] This history of problems with Guantanamo Bay supports the years of dissenting opinion and leads many more to believe that the time to close it down is here. As President Bush claimed, it is not as easy as it appears. In order to determine if Guantanamo Bay requires closing, it is important to understand the arguments for and against this way ahead.

Section III

Should it Stay or Should it Go?

Keeping it Open

Many people throughout the world believe that Guantanamo Bay is succeeding in its intended purpose. It is keeping captured terrorists suspects from harming anyone and deterring others from committing acts of terrorism. Of course, others feel it is a torturous and inhumane prison. There is no question controversy has and will continue to surround the detention facility. For the past six years, the entire world has debated the value and morality of detention operations at Guantanamo Bay. On 22 January 2009, after only two days in office, President Obama upheld his campaign promise and ordered Guantanamo Bay closed. Specifically, he ordered the closure of the facility within one year, prohibited the CIA from using banned interrogation techniques, and suspended tribunals until a task force reviews and corrects the legal processes.[32] In addition, President Obama has tasked his administration to examine the feasibility of moving detainees to military prisons in Kansas, California, and South Carolina or the civilian "Supermax" prison in Colorado.[33] It appears President Obama will not look back, but his administration should consider the legitimate arguments for keeping Guantanamo Bay open.

First, it is important to remember that there are roughly 250 detainees still residing at Guantanamo Bay today. If the base is closed, the U.S. will still have to house these individuals somewhere, most likely on domestic soil. Since the U.S. cannot simply release these detainees, logistics become an issue that requires open debate and discussion. Former Vice President Cheney claimed, "If we didn't have that facility at Guantanamo to undertake this activity, we'd have to have it someplace else because they're a vital source of intelligence information.

They've given us useful information that has been used in pursuing our aims and objectives in the war on terror."[34]

Another reason to keep Guantanamo Bay open involves the amount of resources already invested in the current facility. The U.S. has already spent a substantial amount of money to ensure Guantanamo Bay meets a high standard for detainee operations. For instance, the government spent approximately $54 million to build the high-security detention facilities.[35] In addition, Guantanamo Bay added a new "expeditionary legal complex" for the military commission trials at a price of $10 to $12 million.[36] Another $4.4 million went towards construction costs for a fence around the radio range where Joint Task Force- Guantanamo Bay (JTF-GTMO) houses their electronic monitoring equipment.[37] Annually, the government spends an estimated $125 million in operating costs.[38] Finally, Guantanamo Bay has a medical facility with a staff of more than 100 personnel, up to 30 inpatient beds, a physical-therapy area, pharmacy, radiology department, central sterilization area, and a single-bed operating room.[39] These figures may seem extraordinary, but the key point is that it will probably cost this much or more to establish comparable new facilities in the U.S. to accommodate the remaining detainees. In addition, what expense comes with transferring them to any of these locations? Why spend this amount of money again, rather than keep the current facilities in operation? It clearly does not pass the common sense test.

Another popular argument for leaving Guantanamo Bay open is that merely closing the prison will not guarantee a change in world opinion. Most likely, criticism will follow Guantanamo Bay to its next home of record. While many claim detainee abuse and poor living conditions, the fact is that these same people are going to believe these conditions will exist anywhere. Former Vice President Cheney offered, "My own personal view is that those who are most urgently advocating that we shut down Guantanamo Bay probably don't agree with our policies anyway."[40] Senator Lindsey Graham also stated, "I would like every terrorist wannabe to understand that if you take up arms against us or coalition members, you do so at your own peril, because a couple of things await you, death or injury on the battlefield, or detention and accountability."[41] These are solid perspectives surrounding the need to keep the prison open. People that hated it before will hate it as long as Guantanamo Bay or its successor exists. Moreover, by virtue of the isolated nature of Guantanamo Bay, it serves as a warning sign for those considering terrorist action against us. Housing the detainees in the U.S. may seem like a moral victory to human rights activists, but it will place suspected terrorists on the soil of the very country they intend to harm. The image of the U.S. will not change overnight with the closing of Guantanamo Bay.

Another concern for the anti-Guantanamo Bay protesters is the legal rights and due process afforded the detainees. These people believe that in order to give detainees a fair trial using untainted evidence, all legal processed must occur in the U.S. judicial system. In actuality, Guantanamo Bay will not gain any more legal sufficiency by moving to the U.S. than it currently has. As reviewed earlier, there were errors executive decision making throughout the history of Guantanamo Bay with regard to detainee classification and military tribunals. Those issues indeed require correction. However, correcting the legal complications does not require the detainees to move anywhere. Once revamped, the detainees can enjoy their due process in the U.S. legal system while remaining detained at Guantanamo Bay. The government can simply transport the detainee to any trial appearances on an as-needed basis. Moving the detainees will not necessarily give them more rights.[42]

These are just a few of the major arguments for why Guantanamo Bay should remain open throughout the remainder of the Global War on Terror. The U.S. spends significant human and economic resources every year to operate and maintain Guantanamo Bay at the highest standards. The facilities are second to none among maximum-security prisons and detention centers across the globe. Detainees can enjoy a more robust legal process while housed at Guantanamo Bay. Any detention of these detainees at Guantanamo Bay or elsewhere will still invite criticism and accusations. To think otherwise is obtuse. What is the opinion of the American public? How do they feel about terror suspects moving to their country? According to a Rasmussen telephone survey conducted in mid-November of 2008, 49% percent of U.S. voters said the U.S. should not close Guantanamo Bay, 32% said to close it down, and 19% of the voters were undecided.[43] It appears that while the country felt Barack Obama was the best candidate for President, they were not as excited about closing Guantanamo Bay. Perhaps they fear having these suspected terrorists right in their backyard. Perhaps they fear the possibility of detainees getting released in the U.S. and committing acts of terrorism as soon as they are set free. They have reason for their concern. According to the Pentagon, 61 former detainees from Guantanamo Bay allegedly returned to terrorism after their release.[44] The Pentagon confirmed that 18 detainees returned to the fight while they suspect 43 other have as well.[45] Given these statistics, the American public may feel it is too risky to bring detainees to our soil. If America suffered an attack from suspected terrorists set free in the U.S. after moving here from Guantanamo Bay, repairing our image in the world will be the least of our worries.

Closing it Down

Like any controversial issue, there are also arguments on the side of the opposition. Guantanamo Bay is the proverbial elephant in the room. Many activist and human rights groups around the world spent the last six years protesting the Bush administration's policy and actions regarding detainee operations. Some argue simply to do so and others have reasonable arguments. While there are countless areas of concern according to these different groups, there are three common arguments around the world for closing down the operation. The first main argument comes from the legal black hole that exists at Guantanamo Bay. As mentioned earlier, the Bush administration began this detention operation without a thorough understanding of how to treat detainees under the Geneva Conventions and with regard to legal due process. Originally, the U.S. did not recognize the Taliban or al Qaida as falling under the protection of the Geneva Conventions. Eventually, Bush declared that Taliban fighters were eligible for these protections, but still withheld them from al Qaida.[46] Subsequently, the Deputy Secretary of Defense issued a memorandum in July 2006 declaring al Qaida eligible for the application of the Geneva Conventions.[47] Up until these accommodations, detainees were without POW status. Although the U.S. eventually resolved these issues, there remained a legal vacuum for the detainees. As mentioned earlier, the Bush administration faced legal battles on behalf of certain detainees. The results of these Supreme Court decisions finally allowed detainees the right to *habeas corpus*. While *Boumediene v. Bush* gave detainees more due process power, there remains a misguided military commissions process that President Obama must correct. These, along with the CSRTs and ARBs portray a mockery of the American judicial system, military or civilian. The U.S. incarcerated these detainees without charge. According to an Armed Services Committee report, Guantanamo Bay offered a place where the U.S. could benefit without the detainees having the opportunity to contest.[48] Many believe that the U.S. criminal justice system

has a better track record of prosecuting terrorists than the military commissions. In fact, as of

September 2008 the military commissions produced only two convictions while the U.S.

criminal justice system stands at 145 terrorist convictions since 2001 out of 107 jihadist terrorist

cases.[49] Ultimately, the U.S. fell short by ineffectively applying the Geneva Conventions and by

its botched legal processes afforded to detainees.

Another strong argument for closing Guantanamo Bay relates to the abuse suffered by

detainees. Amnesty International sees Guantanamo Bay as a "symbol of injustice and abuse".[50]

Many throughout the world feel the same way. Detainee abuse is alleged by the detainees

themselves and documented in lawyer's notes, FBI memos, and court affidavits.[51] Accusations

of detainee abuse stretch all the way back to the Camp X-Ray days of Guantanamo Bay. No one

will forget those horrible and degrading pictures. According to a Physicians for Human Rights

advocacy group, detainees suffered from sleep deprivation, beatings, forced nakedness, electric

shocks, and sexual assault.[52] This group also found evidence that detainees were subjected to

stress positions, often for prolonged periods.[53] These are but a few accounts from one of many

organizations across the globe that believe detainees suffered abuse routinely throughout their

internment. Unfortunately, the former Vice President recently substantiated these arguments by

claiming that waterboarding is an acceptable interrogation technique to coerce information from

detainees. He specifically mentioned his approval of this method on Khalid Sheikh Mohammed,

mastermind behind the September 11th attacks against the U.S.[54] This statement only preaches to

the choir of individuals outraged at the thought of the U.S. abusing and torturing detainees. For

detainees entering their seventh year of detention, there is little or no chance that they still posses

any intelligence value so what is the U.S. gaining? One can only imagine that these practices have been employed from the time of capture through today. Factor in the isolated location and "legal free" atmosphere of Guantanamo Bay and it becomes easy to believe the legitimacy of this argument contributing to the need for its closure.

Finally, the issue of America's reputation drives another rationale for ending operations at Guantanamo Bay. Perhaps an unintended consequence, Guantanamo Bay has driven the image of American in a downward spiral. Once thought of as the unequivocal leaders of freedom and democracy, the U.S. continues to suffer from a tarnished image within the international community and here at home. Some fear Guantanamo Bay creates new threats and alienates our friends and allies. Based on how the U.S. treated detainees, terrorist groups and anti-American extremists may strengthen their fight against us. Others argue that Guantanamo Bay constantly drives a wedge in the U.S.'s ability to integrate moderate Muslims across the world.[55] It leads to more anger and resentment towards the U.S. Many feel the actions taken by the U.S. during the Global War on Terror are setting an unacceptable precedent for the future. By failing to take the moral high road, the U.S. is weakening its influence and effectives throughout the international community. President Obama shared this sentiment and made the closing of Guantanamo Bay one of his top priorities. He considered the impression that the U.S. currently has in the world and addressed it in his executive order to close Guantanamo Bay. Specifically, the order states, "In view of the significant concerns raised by these detentions, both within the United States and internationally, prompt and appropriate disposition of the individuals currently detained at Guantanamo and closure of the facilities in which they are detained would further the national security and foreign policy interests of the United States and the interests of justice."[56] Perhaps Obama's swift action to close Guantanamo Bay within one week of his presidency will send a positive message to those around the world that America can right its perceived wrong and find its way back to the top of the international community.

Section IV

The Next Step

According to President Obama's executive order, Guantanamo Bay will close within a year and remaining detainees will be returned to their home country, transferred to a third country, transferred to a detention facility in the U.S., or released.[57] He guaranteed the detainee's right to habeas corpus, directed a review of the factual evidence to determine which detainees to prosecute, release, or continue to detain, and directed a review of the legal processes for detainees.[58] This is quite an undertaking to accomplish within the next year. While it is clear that the detention facility will close, it is not clear what the U.S. will do over the course of this next year to execute this tall order. The next steps are crucial.

At this time, there are approximately 255 detainees left at Guantanamo Bay.[59] In order to comply with Obama's order, the U.S. must first determine what types of detainees remain at the detention facility. The detainees can be broken down into three primary categories. The first category is those detainees that have been selected for prosecution. There are approximately 60 detainees falling into this category.[60] The U.S. must review the evidence and condition of detention for each of these detainees to ensure they belong in this category. This category should include only those detainees of whom the government has evidence confirming they have committed or sponsored acts of terrorism. The second category includes those detainees already designated for transfer or release. Again, the U.S. must review each detainee's file to determine his eligibility for this category. There are approximately 65 to 135 detainees falling into this category.[61] For the detainees already selected for transfer, this process should occur as soon as feasible. This will take coordination between the U.S. and the home or third country, but requires swift action. Likewise, detainees designated for release should be returned as soon as accommodations can be arranged. The final category includes those detainees who are not prosecutable, but still considered too dangerous to release or transfer. Approximately 50 to 120 detainees fall into this category.[62] Detainees in this category are not good candidates for trial due to a lack of sufficient evidence. However, they are too dangerous to release because of their connection or participation in military operations. They are an ongoing threat to the U.S. and its allies and therefore must not return to the battlefield. Once categorized, the U.S must determine what actions to take for each category.

The U.S. should proceed with prosecution for the first category of detainees. There are several options for the U.S. to consider for this action. First, the U.S. could continue with the current military commissions. However, it is quite clear that these commissions were less than desirable. Critics feel the commissions are a "pick-up game" that allow a lower standard of evidence than admissible in normal courts and denying detainees the right to appeal their case to an independent or impartial court.[63] It is fair to say that unless considerably revamped, the military commissions are not the right avenue to prosecute the detainees. Another option involves the Uniform Code of Military Justice (UCMJ). The U.S. could modify this process and better suit it to the detainees. It would essentially work similarly to the military commissions but could offer more legitimacy in terms of evidence and due process.[64] One potential wrinkle with this plan is the impact of the Constitution's double jeopardy clause, which might prevent detainees already tried in the military commissions from facing the UCMJ.[65] It may also be difficult to prosecute al Qaida under a modified UCMJ because of their lack of military

19

distinction, unlike the Taliban. As another option, the U.S. could establish a National Security Court. In this option, Article III judges supervise and legitimize the detention process while the court itself offers a venue to try detainees without burdening the civilian courts with cases or potential security issues.[66] This option, however, is not a very popular one and is seen as another form of Guantanamo Bay. An American Civil Liberties Union attorney claimed, "I think creating a new alternative court system in response to the abject failure of Guantanamo would be a profound mistake. The last eight years are a testament to the problems of trying to create new systems".[67] This type of court could become an effective of means of "guaranteeing" a prosecution making just as corrupt as the reputation of the CSRTs and military commissions. A final option is to use the U.S. criminal justice system. As noted earlier, the U.S. courts have heard over 107 terrorist cases involving multiple defendants and resulting in 145 convictions versus two convictions under the military commissions.[68] This option would take detainees away from the legal "no man's land" at Guantanamo Bay and put them into a public process for the world to witness. Detainees would depart Guantanamo Bay once indicted for the U.S. This would help create transparency in the process by which the U.S. handles detainees. However, there are also obstacles with this option. One obstacle involves the logistics of housing detainees awaiting or attending trial. Another issue is convincing the American public that the detainees will not pose a security threat while held in the U.S. These trials will require sensitive information as part of the evidence, which requires appropriate protection. In addition, these trials will require substantial investigative work and will likely take up lots of time in the court system.[69] Clearly, there are pros and cons for each of the options mentioned above. The U.S. must carefully consider each option in order to quickly and appropriately deal with the detainees in the first category.

For the second category, the U.S. must address those detainees eligible for release or transfer. It seems simple enough, but there are several complications with this process. The remaining detainee population at Guantanamo consists primarily of Yemeni, Afghani, Saudi, Chinese, Tunisian, and Algerian detainees. Of the countries represented, only Afghanistan currently possesses an acceptable repatriation program that ensures the humane treatment of a detainee once he returns. Yemen, Saudi Arabia, and China do not have such good records of repatriation. The U.S. designated 17 Chinese Muslims, called Uighurs, for transfer, but continues to hold them at Guantanamo Bay for fear of abuse and torture once they return to China.[70] Other countries are also afraid to accept these detainees for fear of repercussions from the Chinese. Saudi Arabia has also been a challenge for repatriation. The U.S. figured out after sending many detainees back to Saudi Arabia that they were mistreated. A State Department human rights report noted that Saudi authorities used "beatings, whippings and sleep deprivation" on detainees.[71] Finally, the State Department also found "routine" use of torture by Yemeni security agents against detainees repatriated back to Yemen. This included threats of sexual assault and other abuse.[72] Based on these issues, repatriating and releasing detainees is a tremendous challenge. To transfer or release detainees to other countries, the U.S. must rely on the willingness of other nations to assist in the process. While many other nations criticize how the U.S. handling of detainees at Guantanamo Bay, they are not quickly volunteering to help remedy this problem. It seems hypocritical to hold such strong opposition only to withhold assistance when the U.S. began releasing and transferring detainees just as these nations asked. Some may argue that the U.S. could release detainees within the U.S. The problem here is easy to understand: the American public. Clearly, the Obama administration has a considerable challenge in determining the proper disposition of detainees selected for transfer or release.

The final category is those detainees who are not prosecutable, but are too dangerous to release. Since President Obama ordered Guantanamo closed, the detainees will still require detention. Where can the U.S. place these detainees? There are four primary considerations for detention facilities for these remaining individuals. The most popular is to transfer the detainees to the U.S. Military Disciplinary Barracks at Fort Leavenworth in Kansas. This facility is the only maximum-security facility in the Department of Defense offering a 515-cell prison with special confinement units and an expertly trained security police unit.[73] However, this option comes with strong opposition from the state officials and the local community. Senator Sam Brownback claims that Leavenworth is not the right place to transfer the detainees. His reasons for opposition include existing law, which does not allow military inmates to be house with Guantanamo detainees.[74] Officials are also apprehensive of having detainees in such close proximity to the surrounding community including an airport, hospitals, and farms.[75] Another popular choice for a detention facility is the U.S. Naval Consolidated Brig in Charleston, South Carolina. This medium-security facility has a capacity of 288 cells and has already been used to house terrorism suspects including Jose Padilla and Ali Saleh Kahlah al-Marril.[76] Once again, state and local officials object to moving remaining detainees to the Naval brig. Senator Lindsey Graham and Congressman Henry Brown oppose this move because "moving terrorists to such a militarily sensitive and unprepared area would be to the detriment of the city of Charleston and surrounding communities."[77] The third most popular option includes moving detainees to Camp Pendleton near San Diego, California. This Marine training base covers 125,000 acres making space a moot point. However, Camp Pendleton is not a detention facility and therefore does not possess the necessary infrastructure to accommodate the detainees. There is strong opposition on this potential location as well. Congressman Duncan Hunter adamantly disagrees stating, "the facilities, as they stand right now, are not designed to house large populations of inmates" because "they are not prisons."[78] The final proposal is to move detainees to the U.S. Penitentiary Administrative Maximum Facility in Florence, Colorado, also known as "Supermax." This federal prison can house up to 490 individuals and currently holds terrorists Zacarias Moussaoui, Ramzi Yousef, and Ted Kaczynski.[79] It contains similar features to Fort Leavenworth using state-of-the-art extreme security measures and equipment.[80] Colorado's governor, Bill Ritter, supports the idea of bringing detainees to Supermax claiming that it was "built to handle exactly this type of inmate."[81] However, Congressman Doug Lamborn opposes this move stating that the detainees should not be brought to Colorado.[82] No matter where the U.S. chooses to send detainees, the move will remain controversial. According to government officials, it is more likely that detainees the U.S. will spread detainees throughout civilian and military facilities across the U.S. in an effort to minimize the impact in any one location and making the location a less likely terrorist target.[83] Either way, the U.S. must choose quickly and begin preparing any or all of these facilities to handle the detainees.

Section V

Recommendations/Conclusion

Guantanamo Bay will go down in history as one of the most controversial operations in United States history. Although the Bush administration favored the closure of Guantanamo Bay, his presidency ended with the detention facility still open and American's reputation in question. As promised throughout his campaign, President Barack Obama immediately ordered the closure of Guantanamo Bay. His attempt to "right the ship" within one year will be an enormous challenge for his administration. Likewise, it will challenge the American public as

23

we deal with the disposition of the remaining detainees at Guantanamo Bay. In reality, the problem is not Guantanamo Bay. Human rights groups, protesters, and the media have led the world to believe that gross mistreatment and violent torture is a daily common occurrence at Guantanamo Bay. There is no doubt that occasional incidents have occurred. However, is it commonplace? There answer is no, which is why the problem is not Guantanamo Bay. The problem is the policy and procedures used during the Bush administration to handle the detainees. As discussed earlier, the Bush administration failed to plan for capturing and detaining individuals during GWOT operations in Afghanistan and Iraq. The administration subsequently failed to properly classify the detainees, which led to the improvised legal procedures ultimately discrediting the grounds on which the U.S. conducted detainee operations. To solve the problems with Guantanamo Bay and answer the question of whether or not to close it, the U.S. must change the policy and process, not the location. Therefore, Guantanamo Bay should remain open and continue to house detainees captured during the Global War on Terror. The Obama administration, therefore, should proceed using the recommendations that follow.

Within one year, Obama directed a review of all Guantanamo Detentions, transfer and release of eligible detainees, prosecution as required, and closure of the facility.[84] This tall order requires the president to make many important decisions. First, the Obama administration must review all capture, detention, and intelligence information on each detainee. This will allow the U.S. to categorize each detainee in order to handle the disposition of each individual. The U.S. should identify detainees as selected for prosecution, selected for transfer or release, or selected for continued detention without trial. The last category is for those detainees that cannot face a trial, but still considered too dangerous to release during the ongoing Global War on Terror.

For those detainees slated for prosecution, the Obama administration should try them in the U.S. criminal justice system. The U.S. court system has convicted 145 terrorist suspects compared with just two convictions using the military commissions.[85] Based on the history of poor Bush administration guidance on the classification and legal processes, it is time to eliminate the CSRT, ARB, and military commissions procedures. From this point forward, and in future terrorism conflicts, the U.S. should always apply the Geneva Conventions to captured individuals and treat them as Prisoners of War until they are correctly classified and ready for further disposition. Supreme Court decisions throughout the history of Guantanamo Bay solidified the argument for this approach to detainee classification. When prosecuting detainees in the U.S. court system, the U.S. should take great care in moving detainees, provide security to both the detainee and the public, and protect sensitive information used during the trial. Because detainees will remain at Guantanamo Bay, the U.S. will need to transport them to the U.S. during trial proceedings. Obviously, this requires the expense of operating a military aircraft, detention in a U.S. facility during the trial, transportation to and from courts, and a security detail to accompany the detainee or detainees.

The U.S. should quickly accommodate those detainees selected for transfer or release. This will present an enormous challenge and will require solid support and cooperation from other countries throughout the world. The U.S. cannot do this alone and should not proceed further in isolation. Many detainees remaining at Guantanamo Bay face the risk of torture and abuse if sent back to their home country. In this scenario, the U.S. must depend on third-party countries to offer repatriation to these detainees. The Obama administration will need to exercise diplomatic action in order to garner support from other nations. It is imperative that the U.S. succeed in this mission in order to improve its image abroad and regain the respect of the international community. This show of commitment will restore faith in our ability to wage a responsible military campaign with respect for human rights while simultaneously securing our national interests.

Finally, President Obama should rescind the portion of his order to close Guantanamo Bay within one year. The remainder of his executive order is appropriate and should be followed to ensure the proper classification and further disposition of the remaining detainees. However, Guantanamo Bay must remain open for the following reasons. First, millions of dollars were spent constructing the detention facilities at Guantanamo Bay to include maximum-security centers, a robust 24/7 medical complex, and various security measures and equipment. Second, the American public and its congressional representatives fear having suspected terrorists in their "backyards." Third, Guantanamo Bay is isolated and provides a secure location for detainees keeping them off the battlefield and away from domestic or allied soil. Finally, while the military and civilian prisons in the U.S. are certainly capable of incarcerating an individual, they were not designed to hold suspected terrorists. These facilities require renovation to make accommodate the detainees, interrogations, legal interviews, and classified information. The U.S. would not simply place the detainees among the prison population because of the possibility of retaliation by current inmates who may not be law abiding, but may very well be patriots and willing to avenge justice on the detainees. It does not make sense to recreate an environment that already exists in Guantanamo Bay and for which the U.S. taxpayers have supported.

Guantanamo Bay should remain open and continue serving as a detention facility for detainees. While the stigma of Guantanamo Bay will never completely disappear, the U.S. can reverse the current failed course by following these recommendations and ultimately legitimizing the plan and process by which the U.S. handles detainees. Trying prosecutable detainees in the

U.S. criminal justice system that has proven the ability to prosecute terrorists will offer the world the opportunity to witness the fair and ethical treatment of detainees in accordance with the Geneva Conventions. The U.S. must set and follow this standard for the remainder of the Global War on Terror and for all future irregular wars and major combat operations.

[1] GlobalSecurity.org, "Guantanamo Bay – Detainees," http://www.globalsecurity.org/military/facility/guantanamo-bay_detainees htm (accessed 10 November 2008).

[2] Ibid.

[3] Peter Finn, "Gitmo Closure Called Obama Priority," *The Washington Post*, 11 November 2008 http://ww.msnbc msn/id/27671641/print/1/displaymode/1098 (accessed 11 November 2008).

[4] House of Commons Foreign Affairs Committee, "Visit to Guantanamo Bay,"http://parliament.the-stationary-office.co.uk/pa/cm200607/cmselect/cmfaff/44/44.pdf (accessed 16 January 2009).

[5] Ibid.

[6] GlobalSecurity.org, "Joint Task Force 170," http://www.globalsecurity.org/military/agency/dod/jtf-170.htm (accessed 19 January 2009).

[7] GlobalSecurity.org, "Guantanamo Bay - Camp X-Ray," http://www.globalsecurity.org/military/facility/guantanamo-bay_x-ray htm (accessed 24 November 2008).

[8] Ibid.

[9] Webster's Online Dictionary, http://www.websters-online-dictionary.org/definition/terrorism (accessed 19 January 2009).

[10] Gerard P. Fogarty, "Is Guantanamo Bay Undermining the Global War on Terror?" *Parameters*, Autumn 2005, http://findarticles.com/p/articles/mi_m0IBR/is_3_35/ai_n15674661 (accessed 18 January 2009).

[11] Ingrid Arnesen, "Detainees Not Covered by Geneva Conventions, Report Concluded," *CNN.com*, 9 June 2004, http://www.cnn.com/2004/LAW/06/09/detention report/ (accessed 14 January 2009).

[12] Erin Chlopak, "Dealing with the Detainees at Guantanamo Bay: Humanitarian and Human Rights Obligations under the Geneva Conventions," *Human Rights Brief*, Vol 9, Iss 3, http://wcl.american.edu/hrbrief/09/3guantanamo.cfm (accessed 19 January 2009).

[13] David Linnan, "*Enemy Combatants, Terrorism, and Armed Conflict Law*", pg 153.

[14] Ibid.

[15] Jennifer K. Elsae, "Treatment of 'Battlefield Detainees' in the War on Terrorism," *Congressional Research Service Report for Congress,* The Library of Congress, 23 January 2007.

[16] Ibid.

[17] Secretary of Defense Memorandum, "Application of Common Article 3 of the Geneva Convention to the Treatment of Detainees in the Department of Defense," http://www.defenselink.mil/news/Aug2006/d20060814comm3.pdf (accessed 30 October 2008).

[18] Ibid.

[19] International Committee of the Red Cross, "Convention III Relative to the Treatment of Prisoners of War, Geneva", 12 August 1949, http://www.icrc.org/ihl.nsf/7c4d08d9b287a42141256739003e636b/6fef854a3517b75ac125641e004a9e68 (accessed 19 January 2009).

[20] Jennifer K. Elsae, "Treatment of 'Battlefield Detainees' in the War on Terrorism", *Congressional Research Service Report for Congress,* The Library of Congress, 23 January 2007.

[21] Joint Task Force Guantanamo, "OARDEC conducts ARBs and CSRTs," 9 June 2008, http://www.jtfgtmo.southcom mil/storyarchive/2008/June/060908-oardec html (accessed 12 November 2008).

[22] Jennifer K. Elsae, "Detainees at Guantanamo Bay," Congressional Research Service Report for Congress, The Library of Congress, 20 June 2005.

[23] Josh White, "Detainees Ruled Enemy Combatants," *WashingtonPost.com*, 10 August 2007, http://www.washingtonpost.com/wp-dyn/content/article/2007/08/09/AR2007080900692.html (accessed 11 November 2008).

[24] Jennifer K. Elsae, "Treatment of 'Battlefield Detainees' in the War on Terrorism," *Congressional Research Service Report for Congress,* The Library of Congress, 23 January 2007.

[25] Detainee Treatment Act of 2005, *Council on Foreign Relations*, 30 December 2005, http://www.cfr.org/publication/9865/ (accessed 19 January 2009).

[26] Military Commissions Act of 2006, *Council on Foreign Relations*, 17 October 2006, http://www.cfr.org/publication/9865/ (accessed 19 January 2009).

[27] Fact Sheet – Military Commissions, 8 February 2007, http://www.defenselink.mil/news/d2007OMCFactSheet08Feb07.pdf (accessed 19 January 2009).

[28] Legal Analysis: Boumediene v. Bush/Al Odah v. United States, *Center for Constitutional Rights*, http://ccrjustice.org/learn-more/faqs/legal-analysis:-boumediene-v.-bush/al-odah-v.-united-states (accessed 19 January 2009).

[29] Andy Worthington, "The Supreme Court's Guantanamo Ruling: What Does it Mean?" *The Huffington Post*, 13 June 2008, http://www.huffingtonpost.com/andy-worthington/the-supreme-courts-guanta_b_106993.html (accessed 19 January 2009).

[30] David C. Fathi, "Dangers of a Preventive Detention Law," *Human Rights Watch*, 3 January 2009, http://www.hrw.org/en/news/2009/01/03/dangers-preventive-detention-law (accessed 19 January 2009).

[31] Steven Lee Myers, "Bush Decides to Keep Guantanamo Open," *New York Times*, 21 October 2008, http://www.nytimes.com/2008/10/21/washington/21gitmo html (accessed 21 October 2008).

[32] MSNBC.com, "Ex-Gitmo Detainee Reportedly Gets al Qaida Role," http://www.msnbc.msn.com/id/28800516 (accessed 23 January 2009).

[33] Ibid.

[34] VandeHei and White, "Guantanamo Bay to Stay Open, Cheney Says," *Washingtonpost.com*, 14 June 2005, http://www.washingtonpost.com/wp-dyn/content/article/2005/06/13/AR2005061301513.html (accessed 10 January 2009).

[35] Bowker and Kaye, "Guantanamo by the Numbers," *International Herald Tribune*, 13 November 2007, http://www.iht.com/articles/2007/11/13/opinion/edbowker.php (accessed 10 November 2008).

[36] Ibid.

[37] Christopher Brown, "Guantanamo Bay: A Cost-Benefit Analysis," Research Report, Air Command & Staff College, April 2008.

[38] Ibid.

[39] Joint Task Force Guantanamo, "Virtual Tour-Detainee Hospital," http://www.jtfgtmo.southcom mil/virtualvisit/detainee_hospital html (accessed 25 January 2009).

[40] VandeHei and White, "Guantanamo Bay to Stay Open, Cheney Says," *Washingtonpost.com*, 14 June 2005, http://www.washingtonpost.com/wp-dyn/content/article/2005/06/13/AR2005061301513.html (accessed 10 January 2009).

[41] Christopher Brown, "Guantanamo Bay: A Cost-Benefit Analysis," Research Report, Air Command & Staff College, April 2008.

[42] Spencer, Cohen, Phillips, and Kochems, "No Good Reason To Close Gitmo," *The Heritage Foundation*, 14 June 2005, http://www.heritage.org/Research/HomelandSecurity/wm763.cfm (accessed 20 January 2009).

[43] Rasmussenreports.com, "49% Say U.S. Should Keep Guantanamo Prison Open," http://www.rasmussenreports.com/public_content/politics/obama_administration/november_2008/49_say_u_s_should_keep_guantanamo_prison_open (accessed 25 January 2009).

[44] UScarry.com, "61 Reasons GITMO Needs to Stay Open!," http://www.usacarry.com/forums/off-topic/5974-61-reasons-gitmo-needs-stay-open html (accessed 23 January 2009).

[45] Ibid.

[46] White House Memorandum, "Humane Treatment of al Qaeda and Taliban Detainees," 7 February 2002.

[47] Secretary of Defense Memorandum, "Application of Common Article 3 of the Geneva Convention to the Treatment of Detainees in the Department of Defense," http://www.defenselink.mil/news/Aug2006/d20060814comm3.pdf (accessed 30 October 2008).

[48] Karen Greenburg, "8 Reasons to Close Guantanamo Bay Now," *In These Times*, 12 February 2007, http://www.inthesetimes.com/article/3024/ (accessed 26 January 2009).

[49] Sarah E. Mendelson, "Closing Guantanamo," *Center for Strategic & International Studies*, September 2008, http://www.csis.org/media/csis/pubs/080905_mendelson_guantanamo_web.pdf (accessed 10 January 2009).

[50] Amnesty International, "Detention and Imprisonment," http://www.amnesty.org/en/detention (accessed 26 January 2009).

[51] Karen Greenburg, "8 Reasons to Close Guantanamo Bay Now," *In These Times*, 12 February 2007, http://www.inthesetimes.com/article/3024/ (accessed 26 January 2009).

[52] PBS.org, "Report Details Alleged Abuse of Guantanamo Bay, Abu Ghraib Detainees," http://www.pbs.org/newshour/updates/military/jan-june08/detainees_06-18.html (accessed 26 January 2009).

[53] Ibid.

[54] Jonathon Karl, "Exclusive: Cheney Holds Hard-Line Stance," *ABC World News*, 15 December 2008, http://abcnews.go.com/WN/story?id=6464919&page=1 (accessed 26 January 2009).

[55] Karen Greenburg, "8 Reasons to Close Guantanamo Bay Now," *In These Times*, 12 February 2007, http://www.inthesetimes.com/article/3024/ (accessed 26 January 2009).

[56] President Barack Obama, "Executive Order-Review and Disposition of Individuals Detained at Guantanamo Bay Naval Base and Closure of Detention Facilities,"

http://www.whitehouse.gov/the_press_office/ClosureOfGuantanamoDetentionFacilities/ (accessed 26 January 2009).

[57] Ibid.

[58] Ibid.

[59] Tim Reid, "Barack Obama Plans Quick Transfer of Guantanamo Bay Suspects to U.S.," *Times Online*, 11 November 2008, http://www.timesonline.co.uk/tol/news/world/us_and_americas/us_elections/article5126528.ece (accessed 11 November 2008).

[60] Sarah E. Mendelson, "Closing Guantanamo," *Center for Strategic & International Studies*, September 2008, http://www.csis.org/media/csis/pubs/080905_mendelson_guantanamo_web.pdf (accessed 10 January 2009).

[61] Ibid.

[62] Ibid.

[63] Gerard P. Fogarty, "Is Guantanamo Bay Undermining the Global War on Terror?," *Parameters*, Autumn 2005, http://findarticles.com/p/articles/mi_m0IBR/is_3_35/ai_n15674661 (accessed 18 January 2009).

[64] Wittes, Goldsmith, and Shattuck, "Nuts and Deadbolts: A Blueprint for the Closure of Guantanamo Bay," *Brookings*, 8 December 2008, http://www.brookings.edu/opinions/2008/1208_guantanamo_wittes.aspx (accessed 28 January 2009).

[65] Ibid.

[66] Ibid.

[67] Apuzzo and Jordan, "Obama Plans Guantanamo Close, US Trials," *The Huffington Post*, 10 November 2008, http://www.huffingtonpost.com/2008/11/10/obama-plans-guantanamo-cl_n_142593 html (accessed 10 November 2008).

[68] Sarah E. Mendelson, "Closing Guantanamo," *Center for Strategic & International Studies*, September 2008, http://www.csis.org/media/csis/pubs/080905_mendelson_guantanamo_web.pdf (accessed 10 January 2009).

[69] Ken Gude, "How to Close Guantanamo," *Center for American Progress*, June 2008, http://www.americanprogress.org/issues/2008/06/pdf/guantanamo.pdf (accessed 10 January 2009).

[70] Del Quentin Wilber, "Appeals Court Halts Release of 17 Guantanamo Detainees," *Washington Post*, 21 Oct 2008, http://www.washingtonpost.com/wp-dyn/content/article/2008/10/20/AR2008102003495.html (accessed 21 October 2008).

[71] Tim Golden, "U.S. Says It Fears Detainee Abuse in Repatriation," *The New York Times*, 30 April 2006, http://www.nytimes.com/2006/04/30/world/30gitmo.html (accessed 10 November 2008).

[72] Ibid.

[73] Sophia Yan, "If Not Gitmo, Then Where Should Detainees Be Held?" *Time*, 24 January 2009, http://www.time.com/time/nation/article/0,8599,1873669,00 html (accessed 24 January 2009).

[74] John Richmeier, "Officials Argue Against Detainees at Fort," *Leavenworth Times*, 5 December 2008, http://www.leavenworthtimes.com/state_news/x1049844124/Officials-argue-against-detainees-at-fort (accessed 14 January 2009).

[75] Sophia Yan, "If Not Gitmo, Then Where Should Detainees Be Held?" *Time*, 24 January 2009, http://www.time.com/time/nation/article/0,8599,1873669,00 html (accessed 24 January 2009).

[76] Ibid.

[77] Yvonne Wenger, "Graham, Brown Say Navy Brig Would Not be Appropriate Site Detainees," *The Post and Courier*, 19 January 2009, http://www.charleston net/news/2009/jan/19/no_detainees_here_lawmakers_say68838/ (accessed 28 January 2009).

[78] Sophia Yan, "If Not Gitmo, Then Where Should Detainees Be Held?" *Time*, 24 January 2009, http://www.time.com/time/nation/article/0,8599,1873669,00 html (accessed 24 January 2009).

[79] Ibid.

[80] Ibid.

[81] Kyle Clark, "Ritter Favors Bringing Detainees to Supermax," *The Denver Post*, 23 January 2009, http://www.denverpost.com/news/ci_11533761 (accessed 28 January 2009).

[82] Ibid.

[83] Mazzetti and Shane, "Where Will Detainees From Guantanamo Go?" *The New York Times*, 24 January 2009, http://www.nytimes.com/2009/01/24/us/politics/24intel.html (accessed 24 January 2009).

[84] President Barack Obama, "Executive Order-Review and Disposition of Individuals Detained at Guantanamo Bay Naval Base and Closure of Detention Facilities," http://www.whitehouse.gov/the_press_office/ClosureOfGuantanamoDetentionFacilities/ (accessed 26 January 2009).

[85] Sarah E. Mendelson, "Closing Guantanamo," *Center for Strategic & International Studies*, September 2008, http://www.csis.org/media/csis/pubs/080905_mendelson_guantanamo_web.pdf (accessed 10 January 2009).

Bibliography

"49% Say U.S. Should Keep Guantanamo Prison Open." *Rasmussenreports.com.* November 24, 2008. http://www.rasmussenreports.com/public_content/politics/obama_administration/ november_2008/49_say_u_s_should_keep_guantanamo_prison_open (accessed January 25, 2009).

"61 Reasons GITMO Needs to Stay Open." *UScarry.com.* January 13, 2009. http://www.usacarry.com/forums/off-topic/5974-61-reasons-gitmo-needs-stay-open.html (accessed January 23, 2009).

Apuzzo, Matt, and Lara Jakes Jordan. "Obama Plans Guantanamo Close, U.S. Trials." *The Huffington Post.* November 10, 2008. http://www.huffingtonpost.com/2008/11/10/obama -plans-guantanamo-cl_n_142593.html (accessed November 10, 2008).

Arnesen, Ingrid. "Detainees Not Covered by Geneva Conventions, Report Concluded." *CNN.com.* June 9, 2004. http://www.cnn.com/2004/LAW/06/09/detention.report/ (accessed January 14, 2009).

Bowker, David, and David Kaye. "Guantanamo by the Numbers." *International Herald Tribune.* November 13, 2007. http://www.iht.com/articles/2007/11/13/opinion/edbowker.php (accessed November 10, 2008).

Brown, Christopher. *Guantanamo Bay: A Cost-Benefit Analysis.* Maxwell AFB, April 2008.

Chlopak, Erin. "Dealing with the Detainees at Guantanamo Bay: Humanitarian and Human Rights Obligations Under the Geneva Conventions." *Human Rights Brief.* Issue 3 Volume 9. http://www.wcl.american.edu/hrbrief/09/3guantanamo.cfm (accessed January 19, 2009).

Clark, Kyle. "Ritter Favors Bringing Detainees to Supermax." *The Denver Post.* January 23, 2009. http://www.denverpost.com/news/ci_11533761 (accessed January 28, 2009).

"Detainee Treatment Act of 2005." *Council on Foreign Relations.* December 30, 2005. http://www.cfr.org/publication/9865 (accessed January 19, 2009).

"Detention and Imprisonment." *Amnesty International.* http://www.amnesty.org/en/detention (accessed January 26, 2009).

Elsae, Jennifer K. *Detainees at Guantanamo Bay.* Congressional Research Service Report for Congress, Congressional Research Service, 2005.

Elsae, Jennifer K. *Treatment of 'Battlefield Detainees' in the War on Terrorism.* Congressional Research Service Report for Congress, Congressional Research Service, 2007.

"Ex-Gitmo Detainee Reportedly Gets al Qaida Role." *MSNBC.com.* January 23, 2009. http://www.msnbc.msn.com/id/28800516/ (accessed January 23, 2009).

"Fact Sheet - Military Commissions." *Defenselink.mil.* February 8, 2007. http://www.defenselink.mil/news/Aug2007/OMC%20Fact%20Sheet%20Aug%2007.pdf (accessed January 19, 2009).

Fathi, David C. "Dangers of a Preventive Detention Law." *Human Rights Watch.* January 3, 2009. http://www.hrw.org/en/news/2009/01/03/dangers-preventive-detention-law (accessed January 19, 2009).

Finn, Peter. "The Washington Post." November 11, 2008. http://www.msnbc.msn.com/id/27671641 (accessed November 11, 2008).

Fogarty, Gerard. "Is Guantanamo Undermining the Global War on Terror?" *Parameters.* Autumn 2005. http://findarticles.com/p/articles/mi_m0IBR/is_3_35/ai_n15674661 (accessed January 18, 2009).

GlobalSecurity.org. *Guantanamo Bay - Camp X-Ray.* http://www.globalsecurity.org/military/facility/guantanamo-bay_x-ray.htm (accessed November 24, 2008).

GlobalSecurity.org. *Guantanamo Bay - Detainees.* http://www.globalsecurity.org/military/facility/guantanamobay_detainees.htm (accessed November 10, 2008).

GlobalSecurity.org. *Joint Task Force 170.* http://www.globalsecurity.org/military/agency/dod/jtf-170.htm (accessed January 19, 2009).

Golden, Tim. "U.S. Says it Fears Detainee Abuse in Repatriation." *The New York Times.* April 30, 2006. http://www.nytimes.com/2006/04/30/world/30gitmo.html (accessed November 10, 2008).

Greenburg, Karen. "8 Reasons to Close Guantanamo Bay Now." *In These Times.* February 12, 2007. http://www.inthesetimes.com/article/3024/ (accessed January 26, 2009).

Guantanamo, Joint Task Force. "OARDEC Conducts ARBs and CSRTs." June 9, 2008. http://www.jtfgtmo.southcom.mil/storyarchive/2008/June/060908-oardec.html (accessed November 12, 2008).

Guantanamo, Joint Task Force. "Virtual Tour-Detainee Hospital." http://www.jtfgtmo.southcom.mil/virtualvisit/detainee_hospital.html (accessed January 25, 2009).

Gude, Ken. "How to Close Guantanamo." *Center for American Progress.* June 2008.

http://www.americanprogress.org/issues/2008/06/pdf/guantanamo.pdf (accessed January 10, 2009).

International Committee of the Red Cross. *Convention III Relative to the Treatment of Prisoners of War, Geneva.* http://www.icrc.org/ihl.nsf/7c4d08d9b287a42141256739003e636b/6fef854a3517b75ac 25641e004a9e68 (accessed January 19, 2009).

Karl, Jonathon. "Exclusive: Cheney Holds Hard-Line Stance." *ABC World News.* December 15, 2008. http://abcnews.go.com/WN/Story?id=6464919&page=1 (accessed January 26, 2009).

"Legal Analysis: Boumediene v. Bush/Al Odah v. United States." *Center for Constitutional Rights.* http://www.ccrjustice.org/learn-more/faqs/legal-analysis:-boumediene-v.-bush/al-odah-v.-united-states (accessed January 19, 2009).

Linnan, David. *Enemy Combatants, Terrorism, and Armed Conflict Law.* Westport: Praeger Security International, 2008.

Mazetti, Mark, and Scott Shane. "Where Will Detainees From Guantanamo Go?" *The New York Times.* January 24, 2009. http://www.nytimes.com/2009/01/24/us/politics/24intel.html (accessed January 24, 2009).

Mendelson, Sarah. "Closing Guantanamo - From Bumper Sticker to Blueprint." *Center For Strategic & International Studies.* September 2008. http://www.csis.org/media/csis/pubs/080905_mendelson_guantanamo_web.pdf (accessed January 10, 2009).

"Military Commissions Act of 2006." *Council on Foreign Relations.* October 17, 2006. http://www.cfr.org/publication/9865 (accessed January 19, 2009).

Myers, Steven Lee. "Bush Decides to Keep Guantanamo Open." *New York Times.* October 21, 2008. http://www.nytimes.com/2008/10/21/washington/21gitmo.html (accessed October 21, 2008).

President of the United States. "Executive Order." *Review and Disposition of Individuals Detained at Guantanamo Bay Naval Base and Closure of Detention Facilities.* Washington D.C.: The White House, January 22, 2009.

President of the United States. "Humane Treatment of al Qaeda and Taliban Detainees." Washington D.C.: The White House, February 7, 2002.

Reid, Tim. "Barack Obama Plans Quick Transfer of Guantanamo Bay Suspects to U.S." *Times Online.* November 11, 2008. http://www.timesonline.co.uk/tol/news/world/

us_and_americas/us_elections/article512628.ece (accessed November 11, 2008).

"Report Details Alleged Abuse of Guantanamo Bay, Abu Ghraib Detainees." *PBS.org.* June 18, 2008. http://www.pbs.org/newshour/updates/military/jan-june08/detainees_06-18.html (accessed January 26, 2009).

Richmeier, John. "Officials Argue Against Detainees at Fort." *Leavenworth Times.* December 5, 2008. http://www.leavenworthtimes.com/state_news/x1049844124/Officials-argue against-detainees-at-fort (accessed January 14, 2009).

Secretary of Defense. "Application of Common Article 3 of the Geneva Conventions to the Treatment of Detainees in the Department of Defense." *DefenseLink.mil.* July 7, 2006. http://www.defenselink.mil/news/aug2006/d20060814comm3.pdf (accessed October 30, 2008).

Spencer, Jack, Ariel Cohen, Jim Phillips, and Alane Kochems. "No Good Reason to Close Gitmo." *The Heritage Foundation.* June 14, 2005. http://www.heritage.org/Research/HomelandSecurity/wm763.cfm (accessed January 20, 2009).

VandeHei, Jim, and Josh White. "Guantanamo Bay to Stay Open, Cheney Says." *WashingtonPost.com.* June 14, 2005. http://www.washingtonpost.com/wp dyn/content/article/2005/06/13/AR2005061301513.html (accessed January 10, 2009).

Visit to Guantanamo Bay. Second Report of Session 2006-2007, London: House of Commons Foreign Affairs Committee, 2006.

"Webster's Online Dictionary." http://www.websters-online-dictionary.org/definition/terrorism (accessed January 19, 2009).

Wenger, Yvonne. "Graham, Brown Say Navy Brig Would Not Be Appropriate Site Detainees." *The Post and Courier.* January 19, 2009. http://www.charleston.net/news/2009/jan/19/no_detainees_here_lawmakers_say68838/ (accessed January 28, 2009).

White, Josh. "Detainees Ruled Enemy Combatants." *WashingtonPost.com.* August 10, 2007. http://www.washingtonpost.com/wp dyn/content/article/2007/08/09/AR2007080900692.html (accessed November 11, 2008).

Wilber, Del Quentin. "Appeals Court Halts Release of 17 Guantanamo Detainees." *The Washington Post.* October 21, 2008. http://www.washingtonpost.com/wp dyn/content/article/2008/10/20/AR2008102003495.html (accessed October 21, 2008).

Wittes, Benjamin, Jack L. Goldsmith, and Henry L. Shattuck. "Nuts and Deadbolts: A Blueprint for the Closure of Guantanamo Bay." *Brookings.* December 8, 2008.

http://www.brookings.edu/opinions/2008/1208_guantanamo_wittes.aspx (accessed January 28, 2009).

Worthington, Andy. "The Supreme Court's Guantanamo Ruling: What Does it Mean?" *The Huffington Post.* June 13, 2008. http://www.huffingtonpost.com/andy-worthington/the supreme-courts-guanta_b_106993.html (accessed January 19, 2009).

Yan, Sophia. "If Not Gitmo, Then Where Should Detainees Be Held?" *Time.* January 24, 2009. http://www.time.com/time/nation/article/0,8599,1873669,00.html (accessed January 24, 2009).